This book belongs to

Piper Moore

....

Эта книга принадлежит

Пайпер Мур

....

For Keano, Teanna and Ronomi,
my precious children

What Is My Little One Called?

Как Зовут Моего Малыша?

English-Russian Bilingual Book For Children

Книга для детей на английском и русском языках

Illustrated by Olga Ritchie

Written and translated by Olga Ritchie

I am a hen.
My little one is called
a chick.

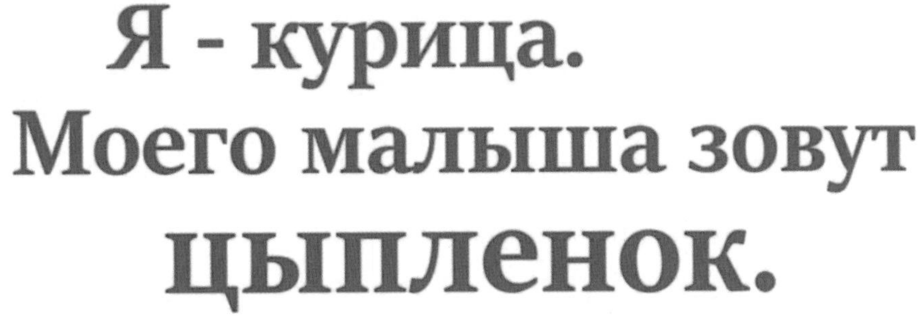

Я - курица.
Моего малыша зовут
цыпленок.

I am a cat.
My little one is called a kitten.

Я - кошка. Моего малыша зовут котенок.

I am a dog.
My little one is called
a puppy.

Я - собака.
Моего малыша
зовут **щенок.**

I am a duck.
My little one is called
a duckling.

Я - утка.
Моего малыша зовут
утенок.

I am a horse.
My little one is called
a foal.

Я - лошадь.
Моего малыша зовут
жеребёнок.

I am a pig.
My little one is called
a piglet.

Я - свинья.
Моего малыша зовут
поросенок.

I am a goose.
My little one is called
a gosling.

Я - гусь.
Моего малыша зовут
гусёнок.

I am a bear.
My little one is called **a bear cub.**

Я - медведь.
Моего малыша зовут **медвежонок.**

I am a bird.
My little one is called
a hatchling.

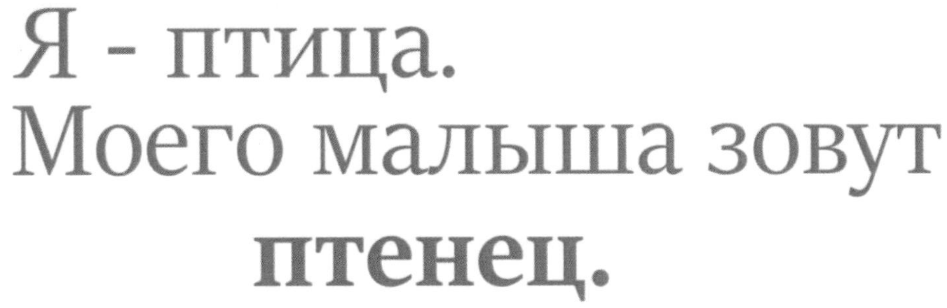

Я - птица.
Моего малыша зовут
птенец.

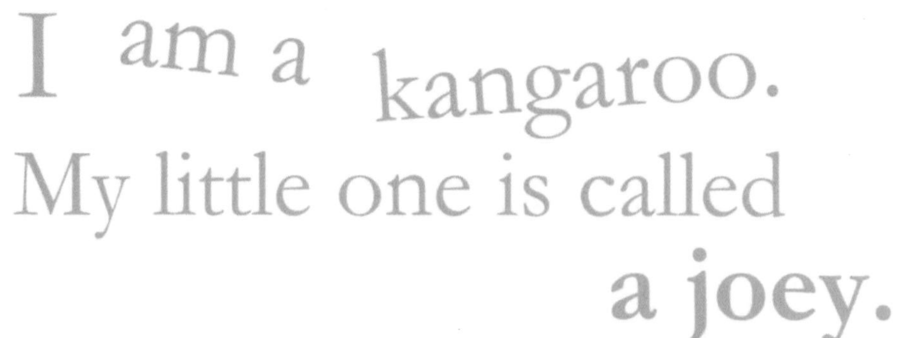

I am a kangaroo.
My little one is called
a joey.

Я - кенгуру.
Моего малыша зовут
кенгурёнок.

I am a rabbit. My little one is called **a kit.**

Я - кролик.
Моего малыша зовут
крольчонок.

I am a sheep.
My little one is called
a lamb.

Я - овца.
Моего малыша зовут
ягнёнок.

I am a cow.
My little one is called
a calf.

Я - корова.
Моего малыша зовут
телёнок.

I am a deer.
My little one is called
a fawn.

Я - олениха.

Моего малыша зовут
оленёнок.

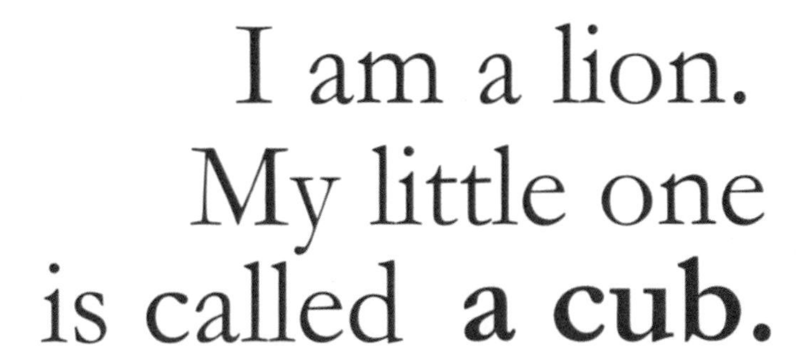

I am a lion.
My little one
is called **a cub.**

Я - лев.
Моего малыша зовут
львёнок.

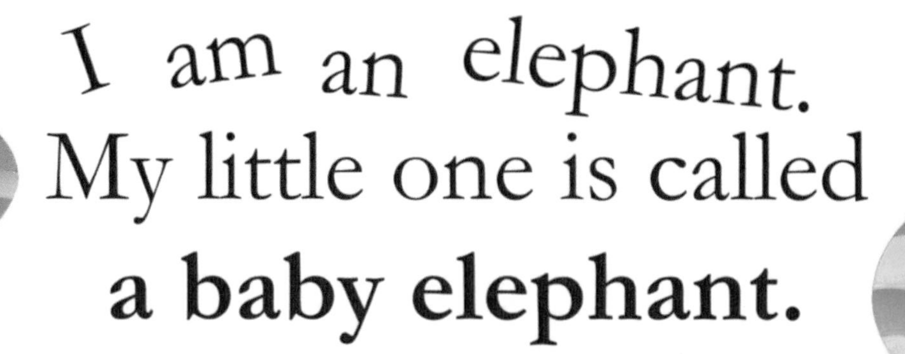

I am an elephant.
My little one is called
a baby elephant.

Я - слон.
Моего малыша зовут
слонёнок.

I am a fox.
My little
one
is called
a cub.

Я - лиса.
Моего малыша

зовут

лисёнок.

I am a penguin.
My little one is called
a chick.

Я - пингвин.
Моего малыша зовут
пингвинёнок.

I am a goat. My little one is called **a kid.**

Я - коза.
Моего малыша зовут козлёнок.

Name the little ones
Назови малышей

Made in the USA
Columbia, SC
02 June 2021